W9-CQV-172

From Eden to Egypt

Studies in Genesis

From Eden to Egypt

Studies in Genesis

REGULAR BAPTIST PRESS
1300 North Meacham Road
Schaumburg, Illinois 60173-4806

This inductive Bible study is designed for individual, small group, or classroom use. A leader's guide with full lesson plans and the answers to the Bible study questions is available from Regular Baptist Press. Order RBP1631 online at www.regularbaptistpress.org, e-mail orders@rbpstore.org, call toll free at 1-800-727-4440, or contact your distributor.

FROM EDEN TO EGYPT: STUDIES IN GENESIS
Adult Bible Study Book
Vol. 53, No. 2
© 2004
Regular Baptist Press • Schaumburg, Illinois
1-800-727-4440 • www.regularbaptistpress.org
Printed in U.S.A.
All rights reserved
RBP1634 • 0-87227-283-4

Contents

Preface

Christians want to obey God and serve Him faithfully, but occasionally our experience sags below our desire. We fail to be and do all that God wants us to be and do. Fortunately God never fails. He consistently and persistently extends His grace and love to us, and He promises to complete the good work He began in us when He saved us (Philippians 1:6; 2:13). Like a master sculptor, He will not remove His hands from us until He has shaped us into the image of His Son. Nor will He stop guiding our lives until we arrive in Heaven.

From Eden to Egypt reinforces our confidence in God's faithful commitment to His promises and purposes. As we study the book of Genesis, we see repeatedly that God gave the human race privileges and responsibilities that it squandered. From the first test of love for Him in the Garden of Eden to the treatment Joseph received from his brothers, we can trace the failures of fallen people. But thankfully, we can also trace the events orchestrated by our sovereign God. He did not swerve even once from His purposes, nor did He suspend any of His promises even for a moment.

As you study *From Eden to Egypt,* marvel at God's redemptive program. Let His mercy and grace warm your heart. Be amazed as you see how He chose weak men to be instruments of His blessing. Wonder at His wisdom and power as you observe His mighty intervention in history in order to fulfill His will. Let all that you learn about God and His ways move you to action. Trust and obey Him daily, and be assured He will keep every promise He has made to you.

A Golden Opportunity Wasted

Genesis 1:1—3:24

"And God said, Let us make man in our image, after our likeness: and let them have dominion over the fish of the sea, and over the fowl of the air, and over the cattle, and over all the earth, and over every creeping thing that creepeth upon the earth. So God created man in his own image, in the image of God created he him; male and female created he them" (Genesis 1:26, 27).

Can the human race conquer disease, war, ignorance, widespread despair, and prejudice? Can we "just get along," understand and respect one another, and join hands to create a perfect environment in which everyone on earth enjoys a slice of paradise? Secular humanists think we can. They believe people can achieve whatever they dream without God's help. As far as they are concerned, we would have a better chance of ushering in the Golden Age if we totally erased God from our thinking.

But secular humanists are holding a badly distorted picture of human nature and a counterfeit philosophy. By contrast, the Bible presents an accurate, undistorted picture of human nature and a clear view of what lies ahead. It portrays people as incapable of constructing a perfect world, but it promises a Golden Age for redeemed sinners. Earth's Golden Age will feature God's Son ruling our planet and dispensing worldwide peace, prosperity, knowledge, good health, harmony, productivity, and righteousness. The Bible also shows that since the dawn of history, the world has been traveling on a collision course with divine judgment.

When and how did the human race get on this collision course? What hope does the Bible offer those who want to escape divine judgment? The opening chapters of Genesis hold the answers. We discover that the first human beings started life in a perfect world. Furthermore, they had a golden opportunity to worship and serve God and to enjoy perfect happiness. Sadly, they wasted that opportunity and forfeited paradise.

Getting Started

1. What contemporary news leads you to believe world conditions are deteriorating?

2. What do you see as the root cause of personal unrest, crime, tensions, and war? Defend your answer.

Searching the Scriptures

Secular humanists insist that people are capable of whatever they wish to accomplish, but the Genesis account of creation portrays God as far superior to mankind.

3. Read Genesis 1:1. How does this verse show God's unrivaled existence and power?

4. Read Genesis 1:2–31.

   a. God created everything in just six days; what does that fact say about His power?

   b. How does knowing that God possesses such power help you today?

5. a. God created the first man and woman on the sixth day instead of on an earlier day; what does that fact reveal about God's love for mankind?

   b. As you observe the created world, which of God's characteristics do you see?

   c. How do nature's order and bounty encourage you to trust God?

Humans are distinct from all other created beings, for God created man and woman in His image (Genesis 1:26, 27). Like the animals, humans would have bodies; but unlike the animals, they would bear the likeness of God. Human beings would have a spirit that would enable them to worship God; they would have moral consciousness, the power to reason, aesthetic sense, and far-ranging emotions. Also, the human spirit would enable people to fellowship with God, serve Him, enjoy Him, and glorify Him.

6. After creating the first man, Adam, God placed him in a beautiful garden and charged him with the task of ruling nature. Then He created Eve, the first woman. Together Adam and Eve would share the opportunity to glorify and obey God and to enjoy God's creation. What evidences of God's goodness to our first parents do you find in the following passages?

a. Genesis 1:28–31

b. Genesis 2:8–14

c. Genesis 2:19

7. Do you agree or disagree that you and your fellow human beings have a God-given responsibility to protect the environment? Defend your answer.

8. Some environmentalists seem to worship nature instead of the Creator. How do *you* perceive God?

___ a. God and nature are one.

___ b. God is a part of nature.

___ c. God is distinct from nature.

___ d. God is all around us in nature.

People often make bad choices that carry destructive consequences. A child chooses to play with matches in spite of his parents' instruction to "never touch those matches." His bad choice leads to a house fire. Ignoring her parents' advice to drive carefully, a teen chooses to put the pedal to the metal, only to suffer serious injuries in a car wreck. An adult, not content with what he has, stretches a dozen credit cards far beyond their limits. The result? Frustration, a sense of helplessness, regret, and bankruptcy. A married woman with two teenage children leaves her family and moves in with a man she met at work. Her bad choice separates her from those who truly love her and leaves her feeling guilty, bitter, and remorseful.

God endowed Adam and Eve with a will, and He prepared a test that demanded a choice. They could eat freely of every tree in the Garden of Eden except "the tree of the knowledge of good and evil." If they obeyed, they would continue to live in the garden paradise and enjoy God's favor and fellowship. But if they chose to violate that prohibition, they would incur His judgment: they would "surely die" (Genesis 2:17).

In the form of a beautiful creature, the Devil appeared to Eve and tempted her to disobey God's command. First he placed doubt in her mind about what God had actually said. Weakened by this doubt, Eve distorted what God had said. Then the Devil lied about the consequences of disobeying God. Finally he told Eve that God was cheating her and Adam. If they ate from the forbidden tree, he explained, they would be like gods, knowing good and evil (3:1–5).

Eve took the bait. She chose to disobey God. The trap sprang shut. Then she gave Adam some of the forbidden fruit. He, too, made a bad choice: "he did eat" (v. 6). The couple had fallen *into* sin and *under* the sentence of death.

9. What kinds of "death" did this sentence include?

a. Hebrews 9:27

b. Ephesians 2:1

c. Revelation 20:11–15

10. According to Romans 5:12, how far-reaching is this death sentence?

11. According to Romans 5:21, what is the only way to escape this sentence?

12. Why do so many people—even Christians—make bad choices?

13. What specific command or exhortation in the Bible has helped you make a good choice? How?

Knowing they had sinned, Adam and Eve tried to hide from God (Genesis 3:8). But God called to Adam and confronted him with his sin (3:9–11). That would have been a good time for Adam to admit his transgression and ask for forgiveness, but he made another bad choice: he chose to excuse his sin.

14. a. How do we try to hide our sin from God?

b. Why do we try to hide our sins from an all-knowing God?

15. Read Genesis 3:12–24 and fill in the blanks to relate the events that unfolded.

>   a. Genesis 3:12, 13 (the blame game): Adam blamed _____ directly and _____ indirectly. Eve blamed _____ _____.

>   b. Genesis 3:14–24 (the consequences of sin):

>   • for the serpent

>   • for the woman

>   • for Adam

>   • for nature

>   • for both Adam and Eve

16. a. Which statement do you agree with? (1) Sinners naturally seek God. (2) God seeks sinners.

>   b. Defend your choice.

Genesis 1—3 reports several beginnings: the beginning of creation, the beginning of the human race, the beginning of God's kingdom, the beginning of temptation, the beginning of sin, and the beginning of judgment. However, we also discover the beginning of redeeming grace in this part of Genesis.

17. Read Genesis 3:15 and 21. What evidence of redeeming grace do you see in these two verses?

18. Who will destroy the serpent, the Devil?

19. What conclusion do you draw from Genesis 3:21 about sacrifice for sin?

Making It Personal

20. How will you respond to God, knowing that He created all things, including you?

21. What choices do you need to make about

a. worshiping God?

b. fellowshipping with God?

c. serving God?

d. obeying God?

e. helping your family members obey God?

22. How will you show your gratitude this week for God's redeeming grace?

"Good" and "Bad" Apples on Adam's Family Tree

Genesis 4:1—5:32

"By faith Abel offered unto God a more excellent sacrifice than Cain, by which he obtained witness that he was righteous, God testifying of his gifts: and by it he being dead yet speaketh" (Hebrews 11:4).

More than a few parents have shaken their heads and lamented, "Where did we go wrong? How can our grown children be so different?" They know how Kelli and Kim's parents feel: "Kelli works faithfully in children's church and leads a women's Bible study. She is a good wife and mother, and she maintains a respectable testimony in her neighborhood. Kim, on the other hand, refuses to attend church. She has been married twice, and now she shares an apartment with a man she met at a bar. We brought both daughters up in Sunday School and church, had family devotions, and showered them both with love. How do you explain the difference?"

Huge question! How do you explain the differences in some siblings? Jerry becomes a police officer, but his brother Jack becomes a bank robber. Manuel is a deacon. His brother Miguel is an alcoholic. Michelle is a highly respected doctor, but her sister is a twice-convicted felon. Dave ministers God's Word, but his brother Don mocks it.

Adam and Eve wasted a golden opportunity. God had placed them in paradise, the Garden of Eden, and had given them free access to His heart. At first they talked with Him, worshiped Him, and served Him; but then they chose to disobey Him. They squandered their opportunity, fell into sin, marred God's image in them, experienced separation from God, and could no longer live in the Garden of Eden. Nevertheless, before leaving the Garden they received an object lesson about redemption and the promise that a Deliverer would crush the serpent's head. They had a spiritual hope, a legacy, to pass along to the children who would be born to them. But like many parents after them, they would look at their two grown sons, Cain and Abel, and have reason to shake their heads. After all, Abel worshiped God, but Cain committed murder.

Getting Started

1. How would you respond if a parent asked you why one of his or her children grew to love God, while a sibling raised in the same way turned away from God?

2. Read Proverbs 22:6. Does this verse issue an ironclad promise? If not, how should parents interpret it?

3. What comfort might you give godly parents who grieve over a son's or daughter's wicked lifestyle?

Searching the Scriptures

Adam and Eve embarked on a new life outside the Garden of Eden. They could never undo the offense they had committed nor return to the way things had been. However, they could start a family and teach their children to honor God. Apparently they had determined to do both.

When Eve gave birth to her first baby boy, her labor pains must have reminded her that sin had brought suffering into the world, but her suffering quickly gave way to delight. She happily exclaimed, "I have gotten a man from the LORD" (Genesis 4:1), and she named the baby "Cain," which means "acquisition," or "gotten." She knew her son was a gift from God, and perhaps she thought this little child was the "seed" of the woman that would bruise the serpent's head. She could not have known that the fulfillment of Genesis 3:15 was far distant or that the coming Redeemer would be virgin born.

Neither Adam nor Eve came into the world with a sinful nature, but their child did. Cain held potential for evil, but his life could have been crowned with good if he had loved God from a young age. It seems reasonable to assume that Adam and Eve taught him what *they* had learned the hard way: Satan is a wily foe; temptation is powerful; disobeying God carries painful consequences; and only the shedding of blood atones for sin.

A second baby boy graced Adam and Eve's home. This little boy's name, "Abel," means "breath" or "vanity." Perhaps his parents named him "Abel" as a reflection of how fleeting life had become because of the curse.

Two little boys would grow up in the same environment, but they would turn out to be as dissimilar as a choirboy and a killer.

4. Why did your parents give you your name? Or how did you choose your children's names?

5. Use a Bible dictionary to find some Bible characters who lived up to their names.

Like most siblings, Cain and Abel developed different interests and pursued different careers. Abel became a shepherd, and Cain became a farmer. Both brothers had honorable occupations, but one brother was not honorable. Abel honored God, but Cain dishonored Him. When the brothers brought offerings to the Lord, Cain presented vegetables, whereas Abel presented a blood sacrifice. The Lord accepted Abel's offering but rejected Cain's (Genesis 4:2–5).

Abel's blood sacrifice followed the example the Lord had set in the Garden of Eden, when He shed the blood of an animal or animals to provide a covering for Adam and Eve. Abel's sacrifice complied with what would become the central teaching of the Bible: "without shedding of blood is no remission" (Hebrews 9:22). Furthermore, Abel offered his sacrifice in the right way. Hebrews 11:4 comments, "By faith Abel offered unto God a more excellent sacrifice than Cain."

Abel implemented his parents' teaching about the way to approach God. Cain rejected that teaching.

6. What characteristic do Matthew 23:35 and 1 John 3:12 assign to Abel?

7. What characteristic does 1 John 3:12 assign to Cain?

8. How do Abel's occupation and sacrifice picture Jesus' life and sacrifice?

9. Why can't sinners gain salvation by offering God their good works?

Knowing that the Lord had rejected his offering, Cain had opportunity to repent, return with a blood sacrifice, and offer it by faith. The Lord counseled, "If thou doest well, shalt thou not be accepted?" (Genesis 4:7). The Lord warned that failure to do well would leave Cain vulnerable to sin. Like a ferocious animal, it stood poised and ready to pounce on him (v. 7). However, like so many sinners, Cain felt the Lord should have accepted him on his terms. Instead of repenting, he became enraged. Instead of acting in faith, he acted forlorn. Instead of following Abel's lead, he plotted to end his life.

While the two brothers were talking in a field, Cain turned on Abel and murdered him (v. 8). This was history's first fratricide, but many more fratricides would follow. The sin nature had become bloodthirsty.

The Lord promptly gave Cain the opportunity to admit his heinous crime: "Where is Abel thy brother?" He asked. But Cain refused the opportunity and chose instead to deny any responsibility (v. 9).

10. Read verses 10–14. What punishment did the Lord impose on Cain?

Cain whined about his punishment, protesting in self-pity that it was more than he could endure. Not only would he be a fugitive and a vagabond on the earth, he said, but also he would be a target for everyone who wanted to avenge Abel's death. Insecurity and danger would be his constant companions (vv. 13, 14).

Cain certainly deserved the death penalty. When God instituted human government in Genesis 9:6, He said, "Whoso sheddeth man's blood, by man shall his blood be shed: for in the image of God made he man." Why, then, did Cain not receive the death penalty? The first reason may be that God would use Cain as a warning about the danger of disobeying Him. "The way of transgressors is hard," Proverbs 13:15 assures us.

11. What kind of punishment do you see today that you attribute to divine justice?

12. What reason might the Lord have for not wiping out such evildoers as terrorists, child molesters, rapists, abortionists, serial killers, and drug traffickers?

Lamech, one of the most notorious descendants of Cain, was a bigamist and murderer. A chip off the old block, he deliberately followed in the way of Cain. Instead of bemoaning his sin, he boasted. He bragged to his wives that no man dared harm him for his crime of murder, for he would avenge himself with a far greater retribution than what God had demanded for the slaying of Cain (Genesis 4:18–24). Thus the descendants of Cain continued in his evil ways.

13. How do you know that civilization before the Flood was highly advanced and not primitive (vv. 22–24)?

14. a. What risks to our faith do you see in our high-tech civilization?

b. How does technology benefit our faith?

Not until the birth of Seth do we find a new beginning. With him began a godly line that included two extraordinary, distinguished believers: Enoch and Noah. Enoch was a prophet who kept in step with God and thundered the judgments of God against those who were out of step with Him (Jude 14–16). Enoch walked with God, the Bible informs us, and "he was not; for God took him" (Genesis 5:24). His walk with God ended not with death but with a transition to Heaven.

As a believer who was taken to Heaven without dying, Enoch prefigured the rapture of believers at the end of the Church Age. A whole generation of believers will suddenly disappear from the earth, for God will take them.

In early history righteous men and women were a minority, a remnant, whose number steadily declined while wickedness and violence increased. Righteous believers must have exercised exceptional faith and fortitude to persevere in their loyalty to God and His truth. Do similar faith and fortitude characterize us?

15. a. Why is it significant that Enoch walked with God even though he had sons and daughters?

b. How can a busy parent maintain a consistent walk with God?

Making It Personal

16. Like Abel and Cain, each of us can choose to obey or disobey the Lord. What choices do you need to make to obey Him this week

   a. in your family life?

   b. in your work life?

   c. in your church life?

17. Genesis 5:22 reports that "Enoch walked with God." What would you like your family and friends to say about you at the end of your life?

Water, Water Everywhere!

Genesis 6:1—8:22

"God saw that the wickedness of man was great in the earth, and that every imagination of the thoughts of his heart was only evil continually" (Genesis 6:5).

Storm clouds were billowing over Colorado's Rocky Mountain National Park on July 31, 1976, but none of the tourists or residents in Estes Park or other nearby towns gave the clouds much thought. Massive clouds were a regular occurrence that sometimes blew over without giving a single drop of rain. But soon those clouds brought a sudden, unexpected deluge to the area. The flash flood roared down the Big Thompson Canyon, turning the narrow Big Thompson River into a raging monster that killed an estimated 145 people and created $41 million in damage along U.S. Highway 34. Homes, restaurants, hotels, and other businesses in the flood's path exploded into matchsticks. A rushing wall of water swept away cars and crushed them under mammoth dislodged boulders and huge mounds of tangled debris.

A Colorado highway patrol officer rushed ahead of the storm to warn campers along the river to flee to higher ground. Some heeded his warnings; others didn't, and their apathy cost them their lives. Sadly, the officer who risked his life to save others' lives perished as well.

Similar floods have occurred throughout the United States and else-where, but the Big Thompson flood underscores the tremendous force of such raging waters and the folly of ignoring warnings of imminent disaster.

"Noah's ark" is a popular children's toy, but the story behind the actual ark is anything but child's play. Noah built the ark during a period of dismal human history. And as he built according to God's instructions, he warned his contemporaries that divine judgment was imminent. But no one heeded his warning, so only Noah and his family survived the most destructive flood in history.

Getting Started

1. What do you know about the devastating power of a flood from either your personal experience or your knowledge of history?

Genesis 6 introduces us to Noah, a man who survived the world's biggest flood. His experiences can inspire us to stand for God against wickedness and to walk with Him when others are pursuing paths of wickedness and violence.

Searching the Scriptures

Adam's sin had infected all of his descendants; he had begotten children in his own likeness, and they shared his sinful nature. With people living long lives, even hundreds of years, the number of indi-viduals on the earth multiplied rapidly. The population exploded—and so did wickedness and violence. Pressure to desert righteousness and conform to the ways of the world was intense.

In that day, as in our world, humanity was preoccupied with the sensual. The beautiful but ungodly daughters of men were an enticement to the sons of God, who made them their wives. These unholy unions offended God so much that He declared that His Spirit would not always strive with men to restrain and reprove them (Genesis 6:1–3).

He called the corrupt human race "flesh," indicating that people were indulging their fleshly desires without any interest in the spiritual. God limited the time for repentance to 120 years (v. 3).

The children of those unholy unions were infamous for wickedness. They were "giants" (v. 4), perhaps powerful political or economic leaders. "God saw that the wickedness of man was great in the earth, and that every imagination of the thoughts of his heart was only evil continually" (v. 5). All day long people's thoughts were occupied with sinful purposes and practices.

2. What relationship do you see in a public official's immoral personal life and his or her ability to serve well in office?

3. What letter grade would you assign to the media's contribution to public morality? Why?

4. Do you agree or disagree that God will soon destroy the human race? Why?

5. How would you counsel a Christian who claims a loved one cannot be reached for Christ because his or her heart is hardened to the Holy Spirit?

Although the eyes of the Lord looked with disfavor on unrepentant sinners, they also beheld Noah. And "Noah found grace [favor] in the eyes of the LORD" (v. 8).

To say that Noah was a "just man" (v. 9) means that he was justified by his faith in God; he had a position of righteousness in God's sight. To say that he was "perfect" means that he was spiritually mature. This exceptional father of three sons walked with God. He had the courage to believe in God and live a holy life in a world of unbelief and sinfulness (vv. 10–12).

God told Noah to build an ark, and He told him how to construct it (vv. 13–16). It was to be large but simple in design. It would be a floating barge made of hard wood, probably cypress, and covered with pitch inside and outside to make it watertight. Three decks would house Noah, his family, and all the other occupants of the ark. It would have plenty of room, including storage space for food for the "non-hibernating" animals.

Noah did not have to go far and wide to capture the creeping things and animals. God said that they "shall come unto thee" (v. 20). God brought them to the right place at the right time.

While Noah was preparing the ark, he preached righteousness and judgment for 120 years (compare Genesis 6:3 with 2 Peter 2:5), but the people refused to take him seriously. They were careless and unconcerned and thus unprepared for the flood when it came. For them, life was business as usual. They lived as though they had nothing to fear. They were eating and drinking and marrying and giving in marriage. They were occupied solely with the here and now, and that is worldliness. That worldliness, said Christ, will characterize mankind at the end of the age (Luke 17:26–29).

6. When do you feel most rejected by unbelievers?

7. How might a Christian "preach" to unbelievers without seeming obnoxious?

8. What were conditions like when Noah received instructions to build the ark? (See Genesis 6:11–13.)

9. In what specific ways do conditions today parallel those of Noah's time?

10. How do current world conditions affect your anticipation of the Rapture?

Genesis 7 opens with the words, "And the Lord said unto Noah, Come thou and all thy house into the ark." For the Lord to *invite* Noah into the ark indicates that He was already there; He would be there with Noah and his family to protect them and fellowship with them every day of the 371 days they would be in the ark. Once Noah was in the ark, he was secure, for we read that the Lord "shut him in" (v. 16). God secured the door. Outside was death; inside was life. However fiercely the storm raged, Noah and his family had nothing to fear.

11. How would you like to spend more than a year on an enclosed barge with your immediate family?

12. Now here's a less personal question: how would you like to spend more than a year on that barge with hundreds of animals? What images, smells, and sounds would bombard your senses?

13. How do you relate the statement in Genesis 7:16 that the Lord shut Noah in to what Jesus promised in John 10:9 and 28?

The ark floated safely on the waters that drowned the entire population of the world. And at the proper time, "God remembered Noah, and every living thing, and all the cattle that was with him in the ark: and God made a wind to pass over the earth, and the waters [subsided]" (Genesis 8:1). God took care of Noah in the time of the worldwide destruction.

Amy Carmichael, in *Though Mountains Shake,* said that when something painful happened to Andrew Murray of South Africa, he spent time in quiet with the Lord, and then he wrote about that experience:

"First, He brought me here; it is by His will I am in this strait place; in that fact I will rest. Next, He will keep me here in His love, and give me grace to behave as His child. Then, He will make the trial a blessing, teaching me the grace He means to bestow. Last, in His good time He can bring me out again—how and when He knows. Let me say I am here: (1) By God's appointment. (2) In His keeping. (3) Under His training. (4) For His time."

When Noah and his family stepped off the ark, they must have seen a vastly different world from the one they had left behind. The flood would have rearranged earth's topography, creating mountains, cliffs, valleys, and islands. Noah was moved with gratitude to God and demonstrated that gratitude by building an altar and offering burnt offerings of every clean animal and fowl.

The offerings pleased the Lord, and He promised that He would never again destroy the earth with a flood. As long as the earth remains, the Lord will cycle seasons of the year. There will always be a season of planting, a season of harvesting, a season of heat, and a season of cold (vv. 20–22).

14. What reasons do you have to be thankful to the Lord?

Making It Personal

Although God had determined to send a flood to destroy all flesh, He had promised to spare Noah. That promise must have cheered Noah during the long voyage. He knew the flood would not last forever. One day the skies would clear and the fountains of the deep would stop gushing. A better day lay ahead. Noah, therefore, relied on God's faithfulness and remembered His promise.

15. Which of God's promises to you do you cherish the most?

16. Which statement(s) best describes you?

_____ I tend to forget God's promises and worry about the future.

_____ I believe the future is as bright as God's promises.

____ I believe God's promises, but I feel discontented under the weight of my difficult circumstances.

____ I think about God's promises every day.

____ I doubt that God will fulfill His promises to me.

A Fresh Start and a New Opportunity

Genesis 9:1—11:32

"God blessed Noah and his sons, and said unto them, Be fruitful, and multiply, and replenish the earth" (Genesis 9:1).

You have to admire some couples' courage and hope. We see the televised destructiveness of forest fires, tornados, and floods. Houses lie flat in chaotic ruin, and we wonder how the survivors will cope with the disastrous loss of property and possessions. Then we hear a teary-eyed couple say, "We can rebuild. We're just thankful we have each other." Another couple comments, "The Lord protected us. We can replace our possessions, but we would never be able to replace each other." Such couples deserve our respect. They believe in putting the past behind them and embracing a fresh start and a new opportunity.

Mr. and Mrs. Noah, their three sons, and their three daughters-in-law began a new life in a new environment under new circumstances. The Flood had changed everything. It had rearranged the world and swept their contemporaries into eternity. Now they stood on the threshold of a new era. Would they honor the Lord or fail Him? Would they remember the frightful consequences of sin and the magnificent favor the Lord had shown to them, or would they fall into the grip of their sinful lusts?

Getting Started

1. When have you recognized that the Lord was giving you a fresh start and a new opportunity?

2. How did you respond to that opportunity?

3. Do you believe or disbelieve that the world can end war, injustice, and suffering and start anew to build a world of peace, personal prosperity, and harmony? Why?

Searching the Scriptures

Noah must have wondered about God's plans for the earth, since only eight people were alive. By commanding Noah and his sons, "Be fruitful, and multiply, and replenish the earth" (Genesis 9:1), God was assuring Noah that men and women would again populate the earth. What God commanded, He would enable Noah's sons to do. When Paul wrote that he could do all things through Christ, he meant that he could do everything God wanted him to do; he could do "all things" because Christ would enable him to. Therefore, no believer has an excuse for not doing the will of God.

4. What immediate plans for you has God revealed in the Bible?

5. How well are you conforming to His plans for you?

_____ As far as I know, I am doing what He wants me to do.

_____ I have never really thought about His plans for me.

_____ I sometimes fail to do His will, but I sincerely want to do His will.

_____ I know God's will for me, but I don't have much desire to do it.

At creation God had made mankind ruler over the world; but after the Flood, animals would challenge that rule. Therefore, God assured Noah that undomesticated animals, birds, creeping things, and fish would fear humans (v. 2). That fear would distance wild animals and poisonous reptiles from mankind so they would not kill off human life.

6. Do you agree or disagree that capital punishment is appropriate in the case of murder (9:5, 6)? Why?

Genesis 9:7 repeats the command God had given to Adam and Eve. In both instances the human race was in its beginning phase. When Adam and Eve received the command to be fruitful and multiply, they were the only people on the planet. When Noah received that command, he was only one of eight people on the planet.

7. Do you believe Christian couples should consider the command to be fruitful and multiply as a mandate addressed to them? Why or why not?

8. What do you see as the benefits or drawbacks of having a large family? How does your view accommodate the teaching found in Psalm 127:4 and 5?

Genesis 9:11–17 informs us that God gave the rainbow as a sign of His covenant with Noah. It would remind Noah that God would never again destroy the earth with a flood.

In a *Peanuts* cartoon strip, Charlie Brown and Lucy peered out a window at a heavy rainfall. Lucy commented, "Boy, look at it rain! What if it floods the whole world?"

"It will never do that," Charlie Brown replied. "In the ninth chapter of Genesis God promised Noah that would never happen again, and the sign of the promise is the rainbow."

"You've taken a great load off my mind," Lucy sighed.

Charlie Brown observed, "Sound theology has a way of doing that."

Indeed it does!

The rainbow is a perpetual reminder of God's abounding grace and mercy. Should we be surprised, then, to see it encircling the throne of God in Revelation 4:3? Out of that throne proceed "lightnings and thunderings and voices" (v. 5); the fierce judgments of the Great Tribulation are about to begin. One half of the earth's population will be destroyed, and many in anguish will seek death and not be able to find it. Will God show no mercy then? Yes, He will. A multitude greater than anyone can number will turn to Christ, and God will protect many saved men and women during that period of desolation.

In Revelation 20:11 we read of another throne—"a great white throne" around which there is no rainbow. Before this throne stand unbelievers. God will have forever withdrawn His offer of mercy and will judge them for their works. So *today* is the day to trust in the Savior and receive mercy. Tomorrow may be too late.

Genesis 9:18–24 writes another sad chapter in human history. We learn once again how prone human nature is to forget God's goodness, trivialize His promises, and try His patience. Unchecked, our sinful tendencies lead us away from God's chosen path for us.

9. What sins do you find in Genesis 9:18–24?

10. Knowing what drunkenness did to Noah, how do you respond to the issue of social drinking among Christians? Choose and then defend your answer.

____ Social drinking is okay if Christians use alcohol responsibly.

____ Social drinking is wrong regardless of the circumstances.

____ I have not decided about social drinking because . . .

Defend your answer.

Awakening from his drunken stupor, Noah must have been ashamed of himself and his son Ham. Ham had gloried in his father's indecency and told his two brothers about the situation, but his perverse pleasure did not please them. They covered their father with his robe.

Upon learning what had happened, Noah prophesied the future for the descendants of each of his three sons (vv. 25–27). Ham's descendants would become servants to his brothers' descendants. This prediction was fulfilled with the subjugation of the Canaanites by the Israelites and with the subjugation of the Phoenicians by the Romans when they captured Carthage in North Africa. Jehovah would be Shem's God, and the Messiah would come from the line of Shem. Japheth would share in Shem's spiritual blessings ("dwell in [his] tents"), for many Gentiles would be converted to the Messiah.

Noah lived to an old age (vv. 28, 29). In spite of his sin, he received recognition for his faith in "the hall of faith chapter" (Hebrews 11; see verse 7).

11. What practical help for daily Christian living did you gain from studying about Noah?

12. What did you learn about God's character as you saw how He interacted with Noah?

13. If you were asked to teach a class of first graders about Noah and the ark, what main truths would you want them to learn?

Nimrod, one of Ham's descendants, hunted for men to follow him, and he built a great kingdom (Genesis 10:8–10). He led the group that settled in the plain of Shinar. Together they determined to defy God's command to "fill the earth." Their goal was not to honor God but to honor themselves, so they tried to establish a world government and a world religion (11:1–4). The plan seemed entirely feasible at first, because all the people spoke the same language and shared a common purpose. They planned to construct a metropolis and a tower that would reach far into the sky.

14. What parallels do you see between the building of the city and the Tower of Babel (Genesis 11:1–4) and twenty-first century humanistic goals and efforts?

15. According to Genesis 11:5, "the LORD came down to see the city and the tower, which the children of men builded." Bad theology errs either by trying to elevate humans to the level of God (deifying humanity) or trying to bring God down to the level of humans (humanizing God). How does verse 5 oppose this bad theology?

God destroyed the rebels' ability to complete their task by confusing their language. Unable to converse with one another, the builders stopped the construction project and scattered across the face of the earth. From that day on, many people groups began to populate the earth (Genesis 11:6–32).

At Pentecost (Acts 2), God granted the apostles the ability to proclaim the gospel in languages they had never learned so that foreign Jews would understand and believe on Christ. As a result, a local church was formed, and the believers were united (v. 46).

16. We do not need another Pentecost, but what *do* we need in order to be a congregation of believers united together in worship, service, and outreach?

Making It Personal

17. Noah's faith was strong. He often stood alone for God. When do you ever feel alone as you stand for God?

18. a. If someone handed you a megaphone, what would you say to your unsaved contemporaries?

    b. to your Christian peers?

19. How do you try to improve your lot in life without caving in to selfish ambition?

20. How can you comply with the exhortation in 1 Corinthians 10:31 to "do all to the glory of God"?

Abram's Fearless Faith and Faithless Fear

Genesis 11:31—12:20

"By faith Abraham, when he was called to go out into a place which he should after receive for an inheritance, obeyed; and he went out, not knowing whither he went" (Hebrews 11:8).

Picture this. Mark arrives home from work and tells his wife, Jodi, "I quit my job today. Now let's get the house ready to sell, because we're moving."

"You did *what?* We're doing *what?*"

"I quit my job, and we're moving. I don't have the slightest idea where we're going. But I believe the Lord wants us to move. He will guide us to the right place and job."

Abram and Sarai, better known as Abraham and Sarah, might have had a similar conversation in the beautiful river city of Ur in the Chaldees, the land occupied now by Iraq. Abram could not share any details with Sarai because he had none, but he knew they needed to leave Ur. The Lord had told him to do so.

Getting Started

1. Using only one word, how would you define faith?

2. If the Lord led you to move to another location, how would that move test your faith?

Searching the Scriptures

Life in Ur must have been pleasant for the most part, although the residents, including Abram and Sarai, were pagans. One of their gods was Sin, the moon god. Located beside the Euphrates River, Ur offered a highly advanced culture, a wonderful climate, year-round recreation, a beautiful harbor, a large library, and many exquisite buildings. But the Lord singled out Abram from his neighbors and countrymen, revealed Himself to him, and commanded him to get out of his homeland, leave his relatives, and go to an undisclosed land. Deciding that trusting and obeying the true God was worth far more than worshiping false gods, Abram left behind Ur and all its comforts.

He did not depart alone, though. His wife, Sarai; his father, Terah; and his nephew Lot accompanied him. The entourage faced a six-hundred-mile journey to Canaan. First it would take them two hundred miles northwest to Haran before leading southwest four hundred miles to Canaan. By taking this indirect route they would avoid six hundred miles of hot desert travel.

Abram stayed in Haran for a number of years until his father died (Genesis 11:31, 32). Like so many believers today, Abram seemed to be dragging his feet instead of moving quickly to do the Lord's bidding. Nevertheless, the Lord didn't give up on Abram; He repeated the call and covenanted to bless him.

3. What promises did the Lord make to Abram according to Genesis 12:2 and 3?

4. If the Lord calls you to begin a new venture of faith, what promises will you rely on?

Abram was seventy-five years old when he left Haran for Canaan, and Sarai was sixty-five (12:4; 17:17). Do not think of them as old people, however, for the aging process was slower in those days. Abram was still a man of great vitality, and Sarai was still a beautiful woman. With his family, his servants, and his flocks and herds, Abram no doubt moved slowly on the long journey to Canaan. He did not stop, however, until he reached Shechem, near the center of the land (12:5, 6).

Did Abram feel a sense of freedom to be out of Haran and in the Land of Promise? Perhaps he did, but Scripture reminds us that "the Canaanite was then in the land" (v. 6). The Canaanites were the descendants of Canaan (9:25) upon whom God had placed a curse.

Did Abram need reassurance? Evidently he did, because "the LORD appeared unto Abram, and said, Unto thy seed will I give this land" (12:7). Abram believed God and responded by building an altar (v. 8). He was thankful for the assurance that his offspring would one day possess the land, and he worshiped God. He cherished the promise, although he would not live to see its fulfillment. Faith grips God's promises tightly until their fulfillment is at hand.

5. What threat to Abram's faith do you think the Canaanites posed?

6. As a believer, you may feel that modern-day "Canaanites" threaten your faith. What kinds of threats do they pose?

7. Thinking back over last week, on a scale of 0 to 10, circle the number that best reflects how well you resisted the influence of modern-day Canaanites.

0   1   2   3   4   5   6   7   8   9   10

After leaving Shechem and pausing for a while at a mountain to the east of Bethel, Abram traveled south until he had traversed the entire length of Canaan (v. 9). His faith had been strong enough to bring him into the Land of Promise, but would it be strong enough to keep him there when a severe famine providentially plagued the land (v. 10)? Until that time, his needs had been well supplied; he was a wealthy man with an abundance of flocks and herds. God had said that He would bless him in Canaan, but how was the parched land going to support his animals? Either he had to trust God to take care of him, or he had to try to take care of himself by leaving Canaan and finding pasture elsewhere. Egypt was nearby, and living there until the famine in Canaan passed seemed logical (v. 10). However, decisions made logically but contrary to faith can produce unhappy consequences.

8. What decision have you made by faith when logic suggested a different decision?

9. What logical decisions might a believer make that contradict faith?

10. How does Proverbs 14:12 apply to the way unbelievers generally make major decisions?

As Abram prepared to cross the border into Egypt, fear snared him. He believed the Egyptians would kill him to obtain his beautiful wife. He was no longer exercising the faith that had formerly characterized him. Abram schemed to protect himself from apparent danger. He asked Sarai to tell the Egyptians that she was his sister (Genesis 12:11–13). She was indeed his half-sister, but she was also his wife.

11. Abram's deception is often labeled a "half-truth." Why do you agree or disagree that half-truths are sins?

12. Fear of getting fired may persuade a receptionist to lie about the boss's availability to take a phone call or see a client. What advice would you give a Christian receptionist whose boss instructed her to tell a caller or client that he is out of the office that day?

It seems incredible that Abram, a man of fearless faith, could become a man of faithless fear, but it happened. Having compromised his obedience to the Lord by leaving Canaan, he soon compromised himself morally. How easily one sin leads to another! And how easily the failure to trust God in one situation leads to a failure to trust God in a subsequent situation.

Abram was correct, of course, in assuming that the Egyptians would admire Sarai's beauty. The princes saw her and praised her to Pharaoh, who promptly prepared to marry her. He sent sheep, oxen, donkeys, camels, and servants to Abram, the prospective brother-in-law (vv. 14–16).

Abram was trapped; he had to persist in his deceit and accept the gifts under false pretenses. His conscience must have tortured him, and he must have wondered how he could get out of the terrible difficulty his compromises had gotten him into.

Fortunately God intervened to resolve a potentially disastrous situation and get Abram back to Canaan. After all, He had called Abram to Canaan, not Egypt. The intervention involved afflicting Pharaoh and his house with great plagues (v. 17).

13. Has the Lord ever intervened in your life to draw you back to where you should have been all along? If so, what were the circumstances?

While seeking the reason for the plagues, Pharaoh must have talked to someone in Abram's entourage and discovered that Sarai was actually Abram's wife. He asked Abram, "What is this that thou hast done unto me?" (v. 18). Pharaoh had suffered greatly because of Abram's sin and therefore had a right to sternly rebuke him.

What a sorry spectacle Abram had made of himself! There he stood, a man of God, being rebuked by a pagan ruler for his deceitfulness! He was humiliated, and his God was dishonored. It all started with a famine in Canaan and Abram's failure to stay put and trust God in adverse circumstances.

To Pharaoh's credit, he called off the wedding, although he was powerful enough to have ordered Abram's execution and gone ahead with the wedding. But God, Who turns the king's heart as He chooses (Proverbs 21:1), turned Pharaoh's heart to comply with His will for Abram. Pharaoh commanded Abram to take his wife, Sarai, and leave Egypt. Also, to his credit and God's grace, Pharaoh let Abram take all his livestock, servants, and possessions with him (Genesis 12:19, 20).

14. How is it that an unsaved person can sometimes act with integrity while a saved person acts dishonestly?

Making It Personal

Pharaoh, a pagan ruler, rebuked Abram, a worshiper of the true God. Something is terribly wrong with that picture, but the picture can be duplicated if we allow faithless fear to replace fearless faith. Writing to the Philippian believers, the apostle Paul admonished his readers to lead an exemplary lifestyle and to be fearless before their adversaries (Philippians 1:20, 21). To lead such a triumphant lifestyle, the Philippian believers were to be people of integrity (2:15).

Every day we must choose to live either by fearless faith or by faithless fear. Making the wrong choice can lead to shame and guilt. Making the right choice will keep our conscience clear and will gain us not only the respect of those who know us but also the Lord's approval.

15. What choice will you make?

____ I choose to live each day in fearless faith.

____ I choose to live each day in faithless fear.

16. a. What threatening situation do you most need to confront in fearless faith this week?

    b. How can you handle that situation with fearless faith? Read
       2 Timothy 1:7–9 for encouragement.

Choices
and Consequences

Genesis 13:1—14:24

"Lot lifted up his eyes, and beheld all the plain of Jordan, that it was well watered.... Then Lot chose him all the plain of Jordan.... And Lot dwelled in the cities of the plain, and pitched his tent toward Sodom" (Genesis 13:10–12).

First Baptist Church felt fortunate to have Pete and Becky in its membership. This young married couple contributed much dedication and energy to the church's ministry. Pete taught fifth graders in Sunday School and designed the church's newsletter. Becky taught a Sunday School class of teen girls, served as assistant church clerk, and visited the elderly in nursing homes. Together Pete and Becky served as sponsors for the youth group and led a young married couples' fellowship.

But when Pete received a promotion at his software development company, he poured himself into his new position. Longer hours on the job persuaded him to cut back on his church activities. At first he resigned his teaching duty, but before long he bowed out of his other responsibilities. Becky followed his lead. With Pete's new job came the expectation that Becky would accompany him to social events with the boss and clients. So she, too, resigned her ministry responsibilities. After all, she reasoned, a wife ought to support her husband's career efforts.

Now, years later, Pete and Becky don't remember when they started drinking. They think it may have been when they attended a surprise birthday celebration in honor of the boss. But they do know they have not attended church in twelve years. And in spite of their six-figure income, luxury house, and a boat, they feel miserable and wish they could turn back the clock and undo their series of wrong choices.

Getting Started

1. What choices influence the direction of our lives?

2. What precautions should a believer take when making major decisions?

Choices profoundly shaped the direction of Abram's life. He chose to obey God's call to go to an undisclosed location, Canaan, where God made significant promises to him. In Canaan, Abram wandered as a stranger and a pilgrim. When famine struck Canaan, he chose to go to Egypt. He chose to lie about his wife, and the choice ruined his testimony before Pharaoh and Abram's wife, nephew, and servants. However, the Lord graciously extricated Abram from that explosive situation and drew him back to Canaan. Soon Abram would have to make another significant choice. Would he make the right choice this time?

Searching the Scriptures

Both Abram and his nephew Lot were wealthy. "Abram was very rich in cattle, in silver, and in gold. . . . And Lot . . . had flocks, and herds, and tents" (Genesis 13:2, 5). Wealth in itself is not evil, but it empowers those who have it to use it for good or ill. How they use it depends on their character.

3. Name a few Bible characters who used their wealth wisely.

4. What warnings addressed to the wealthy do you find in 1 Timothy 6:9, 10, and 17?

5. What wise attitudes about income and possessions do you find in 1 Timothy 6:6–8 and 17–19?

Lot had undoubtedly profited from his association with Abram. The Lord's blessings to Abram had spilled over to him, but Lot had a materialistic bent. When a crisis forced him to make a choice, he made the wrong choice, and the consequences cost him and his family enormous pain.

The crisis occurred when Lot's herdsmen quarreled over grazing land with Abram's herdsmen. The strife threatened to pit the two families against each other. However, Abram was too noble a man to stoop to quarreling and petty feelings, so he suggested that he and Lot separate the herds and families. Then he gave Lot his choice of the land (Genesis 13:6–9).

6. Read Proverbs 17:14. How would you apply this teaching to a nondoctrinal disagreement between two parties in a congregation?

7. Do you believe a church split is ever justified if the reason for the split is not doctrinal heresy? If so, under what circumstances might a split be appropriate?

We make our choices based on what we have come to value. Lot was ambitious for possessions and worldly success. Abram aspired to please God and trust Him for whatever God pleased to give him. Lot greedily rushed to take advantage of his uncle's offer. It never occurred to him to defer to Abram. Nor did it occur to him to let God choose for him.

Lot did not try to determine where his choice might lead him. Yet in a sense, he made his choice with open eyes. He knew very well the character of the men of Sodom, he knew the idolatry of the cities of the plain (how very much like the Ur he had left), and he knew the Lord required purity of life and loyalty. He simply decided to take the risks involved for the sake of getting what he wanted. So he chose material prosperity instead of spiritual blessing (Genesis 13:10, 11). He was willing to jeopardize his own spiritual welfare and that of his family for the sake of that well-watered plain of the Jordan. His cattle would surely thrive there, and he would prosper. He was neither the first nor the last to swap spiritual riches for the paltry riches of the world.

8. Read Hebrews 11:24–26. What contrast do you see between the choice Lot made and the choice Moses made?

9. Thinking back to the story of Pete and Becky at the beginning of this lesson, how was their choice similar to the one Lot made when he selected the well-watered plains of Jordan?

Lot moved his tent close to Sodom, while Abram settled in the bare uplands of Canaan. Abram had decided to let God choose for him. He would not be disappointed, for after Lot's departure, the Lord appeared to Abram and promised him all of the land of Canaan (Genesis 13:12, 14–17).

10. An old gospel song affirms, "I'd rather have Jesus than silver or gold." Why is it far better to know Jesus than to have all the wealth of the world?

We sometimes perceive a conflict between our best interests and God's will, but the conflict is only apparent. The best consequences always stem from our choosing to do God's will. We may suffer a temporary loss and experience hardship, but the rewards more than compensate for the debts. Eventually we will reap what we sow. No one has ever cheated him- or herself by being true to the Lord and trusting Him with his or her well-being. When John Calvin was banished from his beloved Geneva, he said, "Certainly, if I had merely served man, this would have been a poor recompense; but it is my happiness that I have served Him who never fails to reward His servants to the full extent of His promise."

11. What rewards do we enjoy now if we choose to obey the Lord?

Lot had settled in Sodom, but God chastised him for settling there. For twelve years the five city-states (including Sodom) in the plain of the Jordan had paid tribute to Chedorlaomer, the king of Elam. In the thirteenth year they rebelled. With the assistance of four other kings from the east, Chedorlaomer swept down the eastern side of the Jordan, killing and plundering as he went. They rounded the Dead Sea and traveled as far as the Arabian desert, turned back, and attacked the oasis of Engedi. Finally they attacked the cities of the plain of Jordan, taking from Sodom and Gomorrah goods, food, and captives. Among the captives was Lot. Abram received the news from a man who had escaped, and immediately he prepared to pursue the invaders (Genesis 14:1–14).

12. a. According to Genesis 14:14–16, how many armed servants did Abram take with him to rescue Lot and the other hostages?

b. What strategy did he employ?

c. How successful was the operation?

13. According to Galatians 6:1 and 2, spiritual believers should try to rescue a believer overtaken in a fault. How much of an effort do you think believers launch today to rescue and restore a sinning saint? Defend your answer.

Clearly Abram did not condone Lot's association with the wicked men of Sodom, but he loved Lot and was therefore willing to risk his life to rescue him. He actively lived the truth that "a friend loveth at all times, and a brother is born for adversity" (Proverbs 17:17).

Abram was also a man of faith who trusted God against superior numbers. He knew that there is "no restraint to the LORD to save by many or by few" (1 Samuel 14:6). He was no longer the coward who had lied about his wife in Egypt to protect his own life; he had seen the faithfulness of God in the past and was trusting Him in the new trial. As a result, he recovered both the goods and hostages.

14. What specific help has the Lord shown you in the past that encourages you to trust Him now?

Lot's rescue gave him the opportunity for a fresh start; he could awaken to the peril of living in Sodom and get out of it once and forever. He could put an end to the vexing of his righteous soul, dedicate himself to the Lord, and separate himself from the world. But he chose to resume life in Sodom and would later experience the bitter consequences of that choice.

On his return from Damascus, Abram met the king of Sodom and also the king of Salem, Melchizedek, who was a priest too (Genesis 14:17, 18; Hebrews 7:1). Melchizedek fed Abram's weary soldiers, pronounced God's blessing on him, blessed God for the victory He had given Abram, and received from Abram a tithe of the goods he had captured from the enemy. Melchizedek reminded Abram that the most high God is the possessor of Heaven and earth, thereby fortifying him for the temptation that would issue from the king of Sodom (Genesis 14:18–24).

Making It Personal

Abram and Lot made two very different choices. The Lord honored Abram's good choice but chastised Lot for his bad choice. By choosing to honor the Lord, Abram remained a free man instead of a hostage like Lot. Choices do indeed have consequences. Choosing to obey the Lord leads to a life of freedom, whereas choosing to pursue selfish goals leads to a life of slavery to sinful lusts.

15. Joshua commanded Israel, "Choose you this day whom ye will serve," and added, "but as for me and my house, we will serve the LORD" (Joshua 24:15). How will you respond to Joshua's challenge?

16. What will you do this week either to help another Christian make good choices or to help restore a Christian whose bad choice has drawn him or her away from fellowship with the Lord and the Lord's people?

Lesson 7

Trust and Obey

Genesis 15:1—17:27

"And he [Abram] believed in the LORD; and he counted it to him for righteousness" (Genesis 15:6).

I f you are like most people, you don't have patience to spare. We move at such a rapid pace and have so many things to do that we think we have no time to slow down or relax. We moan and groan in a slow checkout lane. We tap nervously on the steering wheel while waiting for a red light to turn green. Our blood pressure rises while we sit and sit in a doctor's waiting room. Finally, when a nurse escorts us to a room and promises, "The doctor will see you shortly," we think, *Sure he will, but "shortly" usually means at least a twenty-minute wait.* We lack the patience to prepare a meal from scratch, so we pop a four-minute TV dinner into a microwave and then wonder how four minutes can last an eternity. We often eat at fast-food restaurants to save time, and we service our cars at quick-lubes because car dealers and auto shops make us wait too long. It seems only Chicago Cubs fans are patient.

Even Abram grew impatient, as we will see as we study Genesis 15, 16, and 17.

Getting Started

1. a. In what recent situation were you impatient?

   b. Which experience do you find more stressful: being impatient with circumstances or being impatient with God? Why?

2. Read Genesis 15:1–3.

   a. To whom was Abram's impatience directed?

   b. Why was he impatient?

Searching the Scriptures

Often our spirits soar with wings of faith to lofty heights of victory only to crash soon after. Abram experienced these contrasting emotions. Genesis 15:1 tells us that "after these things" (Abram's rescue of Lot, his blessing from Melchizedek, and his refusal of a reward from the king of Sodom), the Lord told Abram not to fear. Obviously fear had crept into Abram's heart soon after faith had carried him to victory.

3. What reason might Abram have had to be fearful?

Perhaps Abram's refusal to accept a reward from the king of Sodom had infuriated that wicked ruler. Would he retaliate against Abram? We cannot always predict what an offended foe may do, but we can predict that the Lord is our "shield" and our "exceeding great reward" (v. 1).

Just as He promised to protect and reward Abram, so He has promised to protect and reward us.

4. Read Romans 8:37–39. How do these verses comfort you when forces of evil threaten you?

5. Faithful Christians will receive rewards in Heaven, but the Lord is our reward now and throughout eternity. Which means more to you: having the Lord as your reward or as your rewarder? Why?

Apparently Abram had more on his mind than the thought that the king of Sodom might retaliate. He recognized that he was growing old and was still childless (Genesis 15:2). God had promised the land of Canaan to his descendants (13:15), but Abram still had no descendants. His household manager, Eliezer, was the closest thing to an heir (15:3). It seems impatience had become fear's partner in troubling Abram.

One day a man shared with John Wesley that he had serious doubts about God's goodness. "I don't know what I shall do with all this worry and trouble," the man said.

Turning the man's attention to a cow looking over a stone fence, Wesley asked, "Do you know why that cow is looking over that fence?"

"No," his troubled friend answered.

"I will tell you," said Wesley. "It is because she cannot see through it."

We cannot see through the stone fences of difficulty, but we can look over them and beyond them to the God Whose promises never fail. God told Abram to stop fearing. Eliezer would not be Abram's heir because Abram would yet have a son. Furthermore, Abram's descendants would be as numberless as the stars (15:4, 5).

6. Knowing that the people of Israel, the Jews, descended from Abram, what obstacles do you believe God has overcome to keep His word to Abram?

7. Why is it wrong to insist that verse 5 refers only to Abram's spiritual descendants?

Looking at himself and his circumstances, Abram had little reason to hope; but looking at the steadfast stars of the sky and the unfailing God of the stars, he had every reason to hope. And he did. Abram "believed in the LORD; and he [the Lord] counted it to him for righteousness" (v. 6).

8. When faced with a humanly impossible situation, Abram believed God. a. What are some impossible situations you have faced?

b. Why is it humanly impossible to earn salvation?

c. What kind of faith does God count for righteousness when He saves a sinner?

Although Abram had already believed God's promise, God proceeded to fortify his faith. He said, "I am the LORD" (v. 7). The word He used for "LORD" is "Jehovah," indicating He is eternal and unchanging (Malachi 3:6). Because He is eternal, His promises cannot outlast His existence. Because He is unchanging, He will never rescind His promises. Therefore all His promises are ironclad. Abram's faith in the Lord would not be disappointed. Nor will our faith in the Lord be disappointed. The Lord had brought Abram out of Ur of the Chaldees and redeemed him. Nothing could overturn His purposes for Abram, not even Abram's occasional lapse of faith. He would surely "give [Abram] this land to inherit it" (Genesis 15:7).

9. What does God have planned for you and every believer?

Abram asked for confirmation, a guarantee, a pledge (v. 8). He wanted the Lord to fortify his faith, and the Lord granted his request by making a solemn covenant with him.

The usual form of a contract in that day was for two parties to walk between parallel lines of slain animals. The Lord told Abram to sacrifice animals and birds and arrange them for the ratification of an agreement. Having done as he was bidden, Abram fell into a deep sleep (vv. 9–12). He did not walk between the animals, for the contract was unilateral. The Lord would make all the promises, and their fulfillment would depend entirely on His faithfulness. A firepot and a flaming torch, symbolizing the Lord's presence, passed between the animals (v. 17).

10. What promises do you find in the covenant recorded in Genesis 15:13–21?

Abram and Sarai had waited ten years for the Lord to give them a son. Unfortunately, Sarai's patience ran out. So she decided to go to Plan B.

According to the laws of the day, a son born to Sarai's bondslave would belong to Sarai and become Abram's heir. So Sarai urged Abram to beget a child by Hagar, her slave, and he consented (16:1–4). In devising this plan, Sarai sinned against the Lord, wronged Hagar and Abram, and hurt herself. Unbelief always has unhappy consequences. Sarai might well have foreseen how Hagar would feel after she had conceived. Of course Hagar would disdain Sarai, but Sarai's willful impulse had blinded her.

Inflamed by jealousy, Sarai blamed Abram. "My wrong be upon thee," she said to him (v. 5). And she dared to call on the Lord to judge between her and her husband. Abram was not guiltless, for he had consented to Sarai's request, but the primary blame surely was not his. Abram acknowledged that Hagar was Sarai's property and that handling the problem was therefore her responsibility. Sin leads to more sin, and Sarai dealt harshly with Hagar. As a result, Hagar ran away (vv. 5, 6).

11. What other married couples in the Bible knowingly did wrong?

12. How can believers keep each other accountable to make decisions that honor the Lord?

Hagar was not completely innocent, but she was more a victim than a perpetrator of evil. She had despised Sarai, but she did not deserve the treatment she received. The Angel of the Lord (the Son of God in preincarnate form) found her in her time of intense need.

He asked where she had come from and where she was going. Of course, He already knew the answers, but He was giving her an opportunity to confess her wrongdoing. Then He instructed her to return to Sarai and obey her.

The Lord quickly followed His command with an encouraging promise: "Hagar, you will bear a son; his descendants will be a great multitude. Call him Ishmael—'God hears'—because the Lord has heard your affliction." However, Ishmael would be a source of contention in the midst of Abram's promised descendants (vv. 8–12).

Hagar had seen God, and He had seen her. She called Him El Roi, the God of seeing. And she called the well by which she sat Beer Lahai Roi, that is, "the well of the living One Who sees me" (vv. 13, 14). The living God had seen her and preserved her life.

Hagar returned to Sarai in full obedience to the Lord's command and bore a son whom she named "Ishmael" in obedience to the instruction given by the Angel of the Lord. At the time of Ishmael's birth, Abram was eighty-six years old (vv. 15, 16). Another fourteen years would pass before he and Sarai would rock the cradle of their very own baby boy.

13. Scanning Genesis 16, what do you learn about God's character from the way He interacted

    a. with Abram?

    b. with Hagar?

Participating in a highly unspiritual scheme to father a child was another failure on Abram's part. Instead of trusting and obeying God, he pursued a path of self-will and discovered that it led to an unpleasant end. However, God's faithfulness eclipsed Abram's unfaithfulness. When Ishmael was thirteen, God appeared to Abram and commanded him to walk before Him and be perfect (17:1). A tall order, but God revealed Himself as the Almighty God. His almighty power would supply all Abram needed to carry out His commands. Similarly, He empowers us to do His will.

Read Genesis 17:2–27, and answer the following questions.

14. What was God communicating to Abram and Sarai when he changed their names?

15. What promises did God confirm to Abram?

16. What sign of the covenant did God require?

17. How may God's naming of Abram's son Isaac before he was even conceived have affected Abram?

18. How old would the parents be at this child's birth?

19. What evidence of God's faithfulness do you see in this passage?

20. What evidence of Abram's faith do you see?

Making It Personal

A single act of impatience on the part of Abram and Sarai resulted in hurt feelings and conflict. Ishmael, Hagar's son, became the father of many descendants who opposed Israel in Old Testament times and who continue to oppose Israel today. We cannot predict all the harm our own impatience may cause. It is wise, therefore, to trust God to fulfill His promises to us according to His schedule.

21. What acts of impatience do you regret?

22. What precautions will you take to "run with patience the race that is set before us" (Hebrews 12:1)?

Lesson 8

Get Out of Town!

Genesis 18:1—19:38

"Likewise also as it was in the days of Lot; they did eat, they drank, they bought, they sold, they planted, they builded; but the same day that Lot went out of Sodom it rained fire and brimstone from heaven, and destroyed them all. Even thus shall it be in the day when the Son of man is revealed" (Luke 17:28–30).

When a prospective homebuyer is searching for a new home, he or she may discover that the house under consideration has a termite problem . . . and just might cross it off his or her list. Only a fool would knowingly buy a termite-ridden house.

Lot didn't buy a termite-ridden house, but he foolishly chose to live in Sodom, an abominably wicked city. We don't know whether he owned a house or rented, but he might as well have thrown his money down a gopher hole. Sodom and all its real estate eventually went up in smoke.

Abraham, on the other hand, chose to live in a tent out on the plains, but the Lord was his friend, whereas Lot's friends were vile sinners. Abraham invested in eternity and received lasting dividends, whereas Lot invested in temporal comforts and lost everything. Abraham "looked for a city which hath foundations, whose builder and maker is God" (Hebrews 11:10). Lot settled in a city that had no moral foundation and whose builder and maker was the Devil. Abraham walked in step with God. Lot stepped away from God.

Two relatives, Abraham and Lot, were believers; but their differences are clearly evident in Genesis, particularly in chapters 18 and 19.

Getting Started

Suppose you entered a department store and found price tags that just didn't make sense: a $35 price tag on a pair of shoelaces, but a $.49 price tag on a TV set; a price tag of $999 on a box of paper clips, but a $1.23 price tag on a refrigerator-freezer. Wouldn't you be thoroughly confused until you learned that some mischievous person had sneaked into the store during the night and switched the tags?

The Devil has managed to deceive people by switching price tags. He leads people to think they are getting a real bargain when they choose sinful pleasure and material possessions. He causes them to think it costs too much to choose God's will and spiritual blessings. Lot fell for the Devil's scam when he chose Sodom, but Abraham saw the true value of choosing God's will and spiritual blessings.

1. What things do some people value that God deems worthless?

2. Why is friendship with God's people more valuable than friendship with the world?

3. What have you chosen that has eternal value?

Searching the Scriptures

God is close to His people. He watches over each of us and hears our prayers. But He does not appear to us in person; nor does He communicate to us in an audible voice. Whatever instructions, comfort, and assurance we need are found in the Bible, God's inspired and flawless Book. However, before the Bible was complete, God appeared occasionally in human form to communicate with certain believers. Genesis 18 records one of those appearances.

Genesis 18:1 reports that the Lord appeared to Abraham when Abraham was sitting in the door of his tent in the heat of the day. Abraham saw what seemed to be three strangers. In the finest tradition of Eastern hospitality, he welcomed them, but his behavior indicates that he suspected that the visit was significant. He bowed low, offered to wash the strangers' feet, suggested they rest awhile, and then served a delicious meal (vv. 1–8). Later he recognized that one of the strangers was the Lord.

4. The Lord appeared to Abraham during the heat of the day. The Lord had dirty feet and was in need of food and rest. Why would the Lord appear to Abraham under such conditions?

The strangers asked where Sarah was (Genesis 18:9). That question must have reinforced Abraham's suspicion that the strangers' visit was significant. Total strangers would not have known her name.

Then one of the strangers (the Lord) told Abraham that Sarah would have a son. Because a tent is hardly soundproof, Sarah overheard the Lord's prediction. Knowing that she was almost ninety and Abraham was ten years older, she laughed (vv. 10–12). How could such an old couple possibly become parents? She would learn, though, that human impossibility is no barrier to the Lord's plans. He reaffirmed what He had promised and asked Abraham, "Is any thing too hard for the LORD?" (v. 14).

5. Think of the oldest lady you know. Now imagine her nine-months pregnant. What thoughts come to your mind?

Like a deer caught in the glare of headlights, Sarah felt trapped by her laughter. She promptly denied that she had laughed. But the Lord hears and knows all. He responded, "Nay; but thou didst laugh" (v. 15).

6. The Lord held Sarah accountable for her cynical thoughts. How does the Lord's interaction with Sarah about her thoughts challenge you in the realm of your thought life?

Soon the strangers turned their attention to the dreadful wicked-ness of Sodom and its twin city, Gomorrah. Abraham accompanied them as they looked toward Sodom. He learned that the Lord planned to destroy Sodom and Gomorrah. The Lord did not withhold this infor-mation from Abraham, His friend and the appointed father of "a great and mighty nation" and the one in whom all nations would be blessed. Furthermore, the Lord had confidence in Abraham as a man who would teach his children by example and precept (vv. 16–19).

With great persistence Abraham prayed for Sodom to be spared. He also prayed in full recognition of God's righteousness. If Sodom did not possess ten righteous people, it deserved the wrath of a righteous God. Abraham prayed boldly but humbly; he called himself dust and ashes. As he persisted in his pleadings, he did not want the Lord to think him presumptuous and be angry with him. His prayer is a model of the right kind of praying (vv. 23–33).

7. a. How should Christians pray for those who lead wicked life-styles?

   b. Should we pray for homosexuals and pro-abortionists? If so, should our prayers for them be different than our prayers for other unsaved people? Explain.

While the Lord stayed with Abraham, the two angelic visitors went into Sodom to rescue Lot. He welcomed them and insisted that they lodge in his house because he feared the homosexuals in Sodom. His fears were fully justified, for they surrounded his house as soon as they heard about the two new men in the city. They wanted to "know" them sexually (19:1–5).

Lot tried to reason with the lustful crowd, but to no avail. Failing to restrain the men, he offered to sacrifice the honor and purity of his virgin daughters. "Do ye to them as is good in your eyes," he said. Were it not for the intervention of the angels, Lot himself might have been killed. The angels pulled him into the house and struck the men with blindness so they could not see the door to break it down (vv. 6–11).

Lot had been too tolerant of Sodom's gross sins. Although he had been vexed every day with the lawless deeds of the Sodomites, he had continued to stay in Sodom.

8. Read 2 Corinthians 6:14–18. Does this passage mean Christians should not associate with sinners, or does it mean Christians should not participate in their sins? Explain.

9. Our pluralistic society esteems tolerance. How do you exercise tolerance toward gays and lesbians without giving the impression that their sexual preference is morally acceptable?

The next sunrise in Sodom marked the darkest day the city had ever seen. The angels urged Lot, his wife, and two of their daughters to get out of Sodom. Lot warned his sons-in-law, but they did not heed his warning. They thought he was joking. They would soon discover that what they thought was a bad joke was actually divine judgment. The angels instructed Lot not to look back and to escape to the mountain (Genesis 19:12–14, 17).

10. What evidence do you see in verses 16–20 that Lot had become attached to city life?

The angel allowed Lot to have his way. He spared the small town of Zoar for Lot's sake (vv. 21–23), but Lot suffered the consequences of his incomplete obedience. After settling in Zoar, he was far from happy. Moving from place to place will not solve our problems; we must trust *the Lord* to solve our problems!

According to Deuteronomy 29:23, the Lord destroyed four cities of the plain: Sodom, Gomorrah, Admah, and Zeboim. Lot's wife, lingering behind him, looked back to Sodom and became a pillar of salt (Genesis 19:26). The horror of seeing his wife die must have shaken Lot to the depths of his being. He was paying a high price for subjecting his family to the influences of Sodom.

11. Why do you think Lot's wife looked back at Sodom?

12. How can Christians shape their children's moral and spiritual character in a culture steeped in immorality and anti-Christian philosophies?

The next day Abraham revisited the place where he had stood before the Lord on a hill east of Hebron (vv. 27, 28). He could see Sodom from there. Years earlier, Abraham and Lot had viewed Sodom, but how different Sodom had looked to Abraham than to Lot.

Lot didn't feel safe in Zoar. Fearful of the inhabitants, he fled to the mountain and found a cave for his home (v. 30). He had moved to Sodom because he wanted more room and more riches. In the end he had neither room nor riches. He had become a living illustration of the truth expressed in Proverbs 14:14: "The backslider in heart shall be filled with [the fruit of] his own ways."

13. Read Matthew 10:39. What did Jesus say about losing one's life for His sake?

Lot reaped the bitter fruit of his own ways. His daughters had grown up in Sodom and observed all too well the Sodomites' lifestyle. Their sense of values was so distorted that they thought it worse for the family to have no posterity than to be immoral by committing incest. They made their father drunk in order to have sex with him and bear his children. Shamelessly they accomplished their objective (Genesis 19:31–38).

Making It Personal

Galatians 6:6 and 7 warn that sowing to the flesh reaps corruption. Lot sowed to the flesh and reaped the sad consequences: loss of property, loss of an effective testimony, loss of his wife, loss of his dignity, and, last but not least, the loss of God's approval. Life brims with opportunities to do things that have eternal value, but life is too brief for us to let any of those opportunities slip past us.

14. Record some instances from this past week when you took the opportunity to do something of eternal value.

b. Record some opportunities you squandered.

15. What failures in Lot's life will you try to avoid?

16. Which commendable choices or actions in Abraham's life will you strive to emulate?

It's a Boy!

Genesis 20:1—23:20

"The LORD visited Sarah as he had said, and the LORD did unto Sarah as he had spoken" (Genesis 21:1).

I n 1997 a retired sixty-three-year-old California woman gave birth to her first child. She and her husband had spent $50,000 on fertility treatments that eventually led to conception and birth.

If you find this story amazing, here's one that's even more intriguing. In the Middle East a ninety-year-old woman married to a one-hundred-year-old man gave birth to a baby boy. The child was her first, and they hadn't spent a dime trying to get pregnant. The event didn't get TV coverage, but it has been receiving significant attention for almost four thousand years. You see, the birth was supernatural; God intervened in the lives of Abraham and Sarah—and in history—to give them a son, who would continue the lineage through which Jesus, the Savior, eventually came.

Getting Started

1. Whose birth in your lifetime do you consider most unusual or significant?

2. What blessings can parents expect when a baby enters their lives?

3. What challenges does a new baby bring?

Searching the Scriptures

Isaac's arrival must have delighted his parents. They had waited twenty years for God to give them this son of promise. They named their little boy "Isaac," the Hebrew word for "laughter" (Genesis 21:3). Both Abraham and Sarah had laughed a year earlier, when God had predicted this special birth (17:17; 18:10–12). Sarah also credited God with bringing laughter to her. She must have seen some humor in the fact that at the age of ninety she would be nursing her own baby. So the name "Isaac" seemed appropriate.

Obviously Abraham was a proud father. The day Isaac was weaned, Abraham hosted a huge celebration in honor of his little boy. But not everyone shared that father's joy (21:6–9).

4. Read Genesis 21:9–11.

   a. Who ridiculed Isaac?

   b. Who caught the scoffer in the act?

   c. What punishment did the observer recommend?

   d. How did Abraham feel about this incident?

Keep in mind that Ishmael was Abraham's son. Did Abraham have to banish this teenager from his home and heart? Yes. The relationship between the two boys could only worsen, and Isaac alone was the rightful heir to the Abrahamic Covenant.

5. What spiritual parallels did Paul draw in Galatians 4:28–31 between the Isaac-Ishmael incident and that of the Galatian believers? (Hint: False teachers had insisted that the Galatians must work for salvation.)

God instructed Abraham to follow Sarah's advice, and He assured Abraham that He would take care of Ishmael and make him a great nation because he was Abraham's son (Genesis 21:12, 13).

Banished from their home, from all that was familiar and loved, Hagar and Ishmael experienced the loneliness of a long trek to Egypt. Losing their way, they wandered about in the wilderness of Beersheba. Having used up the water in their bottles, they faced a hopeless situation. Hagar placed Ishmael under the shade of a shrub and walked away because she could not bear to see him die. She wept loudly while Ishmael moaned through lips parched from the desert heat (vv. 14–16).

The Lord graciously responded to Hagar's need. He promised He would make Ishmael the father of a great nation, and then He led Hagar to a well. After being refreshed, Hagar turned south to the wilderness of Paran, where Ishmael grew to manhood, marrying an Egyptian girl and becoming a hunter (vv. 17–21).

Although many testings of faith lay behind Abraham, the most severe test awaited him. The Lord commanded him to offer Isaac as a sacrifice on an altar (22:1, 2).

Read Genesis 22:3–18 and answer the following questions.

6. From a human standpoint, how well did the command to slay Isaac harmonize with the Lord's promise to establish His covenant with Isaac (Genesis 17:21)?

7. What indications do you see that Abraham obeyed the Lord's command?

8. How would you describe Isaac's relationship with his father?

9. Why do you believe the Lord tested Abraham's faith?

10. Why does He test your faith?

11. What picture of Christ do you find in this passage?

12. How did the Lord affirm Abraham's faith?

13. According to Hebrews 11:17–19, what did Abraham believe the Lord would do if he sacrificed Isaac?

14. How strongly do you believe God will fulfill all His promises?

Sarah died in Hebron in the land of Canaan at the age of 127. Abraham sat beside her lifeless body and wept (Genesis 23:1, 2). "The unspoken memories of a lifetime were in those tears," it has been observed. The wife of his youth had been his lifelong companion. She had traveled with him, toiled with him, shed tears with him, laughed with him, and shared with him his faith, his dreams, his daily life. His life and hers had been intertwined. Now death had abruptly torn them apart, leaving Abraham not merely alone but with part of himself forever gone.

Isaac shared his father's grief. For three years he mourned his loss. Not until Rebekah became his wife was he "comforted after his mother's death" (24:67). That Abraham and Isaac loved Sarah so deeply spoke more eloquently of her than any epitaph or tombstone ever could have.

15. What comforting thoughts keep us from despairing when a Christian loved one dies?

16. How can you show your parents or children *now* that you love them?

Abraham purchased a burying place for Sarah from Ephron, a Hittite. It was a field with a cave, surrounded by trees and within sight of Abraham's home in Mamre. It was the only part of Canaan that Abraham ever owned (23:20). He died in faith, not having received the fulfillment of God's promises; but having seen the fulfillment afar off, he was persuaded that God would keep His word and ultimately cause a believing company of Abraham's seed to inherit the land (25:8–10; Hebrews 11:13).

Making It Personal

Abraham had learned by experience that God is trustworthy. As he exercised his faith, it grew. There is no other way for faith to grow!

17. What two Bible promises will you rely on this week to support your faith when it is tested?

18. Abraham exerted a positive influence on his son Isaac. In what ways does your life serve as a positive example for your loved ones?

Lesson 10

Isaac's Dysfunctional Family

Genesis 24; 25:19–34; 27:1–40

"By faith Isaac blessed Jacob and Esau concerning things to come" (Hebrews 11:20).

Are you an order-from-the-catalog kind of buyer? You thumb through a catalog, spy a jacket that appeals to you, complete an order form, mail the form with a check, and wait for delivery. Or are you a must-see-the-real-thing-before-buying kind of buyer? If you are neither, you might use a personal shopper, who will do the footwork and purchasing for you. Of course you would have to trust your personal shopper implicitly. You wouldn't want to dispatch a personal shopper to buy a couple of golf clubs and end up holding costly shares in two eighteen-hole courses.

Think about your buying habits. What would you buy sight unseen? Would you let anybody make shopping choices for you?

Here's an even bigger question. Would you trust a relative, friend, or associate to select a spouse for you?

Abraham dispatched his oldest servant to Abraham's homeland to acquire a bride for his son Isaac. Fortunately the servant was trustworthy and submissive to the Lord's will. The ensuing marriage was a good match, but with the arrival of children, the family became dysfunctional.

Getting Started

1. Why is it so important to marry the right person?

2. In what ways might a two-parent family be dysfunctional?

Searching the Scriptures

In all probability it would have been a simple matter for Abraham to find a bride for Isaac among the Canaanites. But he resolutely opposed the thought of bringing a Canaanite into his family. He charged his servant to find Isaac's bride among his own people back home.

3. According to Genesis 24:1–3, how did Abraham show that he would not accept a Canaanite bride for his son?

4. Read 2 Corinthians 6:14. How should a Christian parent respond to a believing son or daughter who wants to marry an unbeliever?

5. How should a Christian parent respond to a son or daughter who argues that he or she will be able to influence the unbeliever to become a Christian after they marry?

Abraham, a man of faith, assured his servant of success. He promised that the Lord God of Heaven would "send his angel before thee, and thou shalt take a wife unto my son from thence" (Genesis 24:7). Reassured, the servant left for his five-hundred-mile journey to Haran, the city of Abraham's brother Nahor.

Just outside the city, the servant stopped at a well where women went to draw water. He prayed for guidance and later praised the Lord for showing goodness to his master, Abraham (vv. 14, 27). A young woman named Rebekah met all the criteria the servant had outlined in his prayer.

Abraham's servant accepted Rebekah's offer to enjoy her family's hospitality, but he would not eat until he had told her family about his mission. Furthermore, he would not linger in Haran and delay his return to his master after he had achieved his objective (vv. 15–56).

6. What commendable characteristics do you see in Rebekah as you read Genesis 24:16–28?

7. If you were looking for a bride for your son, grandson, or some other close male relative, what characteristics would you look for?

Rebekah's family accepted a generous dowry for her. Then they blessed her and said good-bye. Rebekah accompanied the servant to Abraham and Isaac's home.

As the travelers approached their destination, Isaac saw Rebekah, and she saw him. When their eyes met, so did their hearts. Isaac escorted his bride into his mother's tent and married her (vv. 53–67).

8. Review Isaac and Rebekah's "love story" and explain

a. how it pictures the role of our Heavenly Father in salvation.

b. how it pictures the role of the Holy Spirit in salvation.

c. how it pictures the role of the believer in salvation.

d. how it pictures the role of God's Son in salvation.

After waiting twenty-two years for a son, Isaac prayed to the Lord on behalf of his wife. The Lord answered his prayer with the birth of Esau and Jacob. Although they were twins, the brothers were markedly dissimilar in temperament, and they struggled with each other from the beginning (25:21–26). Their most significant difference involved their relationship with the Lord: Jacob showed an interest in spiritual values; Esau disdained them.

As the elder son, Esau was favored to receive the birthright and its accompanying blessings. He would have succeeded Isaac as the ruler of the household. He would have inherited the Abrahamic Covenant with its promise of Canaan for Abraham's descendants and the promise of the coming of the Messiah. Also he would have inherited a major portion of Abraham's possessions.

One day after hunting game, Esau came upon Jacob cooking lentil stew. The smell of the savory food stimulated Esau's appetite, and he requested, "Feed me, I pray thee, with that same red pottage; for I am faint." Jacob knew well the things his brother valued most and asked for Esau's birthright in exchange for the stew (vv. 29–31).

9. According to verses 32–34, how did Esau respond to Jacob's proposed deal?

10. How did Esau feel about the birthright?

11. What trades might believers be tempted to make, valuing fleshly gratification more highly than spiritual privileges?

12. What incentive does 1 John 2:17 give for embracing God's will rather than giving in to sinful lusts?

13. Are you facing a temptation to value a fleshly desire more highly than a spiritual privilege? If so, how will you respond to the temptation?

Isaac became old and blind. Thinking he was about to die, he asked Esau to hunt for wild game and to prepare him a tasty meal, after which he would give Esau his blessing. Rebekah overheard Isaac's request; she quickly prepared a tasty meal of two choice young goats, which she gave to Jacob to serve to Isaac so he would obtain his father's blessing. Before sending Jacob on this ruse, she dressed him in Esau's clothes and covered his neck and hands with goatskins. Isaac would surely think that his hairy son, Esau, was serving the meal (Genesis 27:1–17).

The ruse worked. Isaac blessed Jacob with all the blessings of the birthright, but when Isaac learned that he had been tricked, he "trembled" (v. 33). Nevertheless, he recognized that God had chosen Jacob to receive the birthright. He would not rescind his blessings, but he did pronounce a lesser blessing on Esau (vv. 38–40; see also Hebrews 11:20).

Upon learning that Esau hated Jacob for what he had done, Rebekah reacted by sending Jacob away for what she thought would be a "few days" (Genesis 27:44), but Jacob would be away from home for twenty years. She also had taught Jacob to scheme. Instead of encouraging him to trust God, she taught him to get what he could (even good things) by unholy means.

But there was enough blame to go around in Isaac's dysfunctional family. Esau was blameworthy because he sold his birthright to gratify his flesh. He had forfeited his father's best blessing; he had little justification for his bitter cry against Jacob and his tearful pleading for a blessing from his father.

Isaac was certainly not without blame, for he knew that Jacob, not Esau, was divinely appointed to rule. Isaac had tried to thwart God's plan because he favored Esau over Jacob (25:23, 28).

14. Isaac loved Esau, while Rebekah loved Jacob (25:28). Although no two children are alike, how can parents show each child that they love all the children equally?

Making It Personal

Twenty-first century culture places little or no value on character and spiritual matters. As someone commented, "People today seem to have gold for their god and greed for their creed." Because so many parents push aside character and spiritual matters in their mad rush for more and more things, they leave little time for the work of parenting. And parenting does demand work. Is it any wonder, then, that dysfunctional families are common and many children seem self-centered and angry?

15. How might the church help families build happy, loving, godly homes?

16. What role might you play in helping your church become a fellowship of loving, well-adjusted families?

All's Well That Ends Well

Genesis 27:4—29:30; 32:1—33:20

"The LORD hear thee in the day of trouble; the name of the God of Jacob defend thee" (Psalm 20:1).

Two brothers in a midsize city haven't spoken to each other in twenty years. Neither brother can tell you when he stopped speaking to the other, but both will tell you they don't plan to reconcile. The emotional wall that separates them is as hard as a rock and as thick as a redwood forest. What is particularly sad is that both brothers are Christians who regularly attend church—different churches, of course!

When Esau learned that Jacob had deceived their father and received the blessing of the birthright, he was furious. A wall of resentment and hostility suddenly came between the two brothers. Tensions mounted. It looked like the two would never resolve their differences.

Getting Started

1. What situations have been known to alienate family members?

2. What situations have been known to alienate members of a church family?

3. Why should believers strive "to keep the unity of the Spirit in the bond of peace" (Ephesians 4:3)?

Searching the Scriptures

Instead of blaming himself for despising his birthright, Esau vowed to kill Jacob after mourning their father's death (Genesis 27:41). That delay gave Jacob time to leave home.

Rebekah urged Jacob to flee to her brother's house in Haran for a few days, but she would never see Jacob again. Not only did she fear that Esau would kill Jacob if he stayed home, but she also feared Jacob might marry one of the pagan girls in Canaan. Esau had already done so; he had married two Hittite girls, who were "a grief of mind unto Isaac and to Rebekah" (26:35). Two pagan daughters-in-law were more than enough!

Rebekah had shared many blessed years with Isaac and had shared his faith as well, but her jealous concern for her favorite son hurt the entire family.

4. What damage do you think may occur when a parent favors one child at the expense of another?

5. Do you agree or disagree with the comment that "God doesn't have favorites, but He does have intimates"? Why?

Isaac called Jacob to his side and charged him to go to Haran to find a wife who was not like the daughters of Canaan. Isaac knew that the long journey would be lonely and that Jacob would have to adjust to a new environment; he therefore tried to encourage him. He blessed Jacob and asked the all-powerful God to bless him, multiply his seed, and give him the promised land of Canaan (28:1–4).

Jacob traveled for three days before he reached a place he would afterwards name Bethel. The Lord met him there in a most unusual way. While Jacob slept, the Lord gave him a dream in which he saw a stairway to the stars (vv. 11–16). The Lord stood above the stairway, and angels were ascending to Him and descending to the earth.

6. According to verses 13–15, what promises did the Lord make to Jacob?

When he awoke, Jacob recognized God's presence; memorialized the place with an oil-anointed stone; named the place "Bethel," meaning "the house of God"; and vowed to be faithful to the Lord (vv. 16–22). The road ahead would not be an easy one, but the Lord wanted Jacob to face it with faith and fortitude.

7. Was Jacob trying to bargain with the Lord by vowing to tithe (v. 22)? Explain.

8. What motives should believers have for giving faithfully to the Lord?

Refreshed by his meeting with God, Jacob completed his journey to Haran with the joyful expectation of finding a wife. There, by a well, he met Rachel, a gentle and beautiful shepherdess. Ordinarily sons would care for sheep; but at the time, Rachel's father, Laban, had only two daughters. Rachel, the younger daughter, had the job of herding her father's sheep. As Rachel approached the well with her sheep, Jacob sprang to the well, removed a heavy stone from its mouth, and watered the sheep. He had learned her identity and was obviously attracted to her. Overwhelmed with emotion, he wept for joy (29:1–11).

Uncle Laban welcomed Jacob to his home, where he stayed for a month. Laban offered Jacob a job and asked him to set his own wages. Jacob wanted to marry Rachel, but he had neither dowry to give for her nor money for the usual gifts for relatives. So he offered to serve Laban for seven years in order to marry Rachel.

Laban quickly accepted the offer, and the seven years "seemed unto him [Jacob] but a few days, for the love he had to her" (v. 20). True love can be patient, and expectation of future bliss can make time fly.

9. According to verses 21–27, how did Laban scam Jacob?

10. How did Jacob respond?

11. How has someone you trusted disappointed you, perhaps even cheated you?

12. How should you, as a believer, respond when someone cheats you?

After twenty years with Uncle Laban in Haran, at the Lord's command Jacob began the long journey back to Canaan (31:3). Unsure of how Esau would receive him, he was apprehensive. But the Lord took command of the situation. He intercepted Jacob with a host of angels.

Jacob was not totally reassured by his company of angels, so he dispatched messengers to find Esau and solicit his favor. The messengers returned with the unsettling news that Esau and four hundred soldiers were on their way to meet Jacob. "Then," the Bible tells us, "Jacob was greatly afraid and distressed" (32:7). He prayed for deliverance and sent droves of animals as a gift to Esau in an effort to quiet his anger and secure his favor (vv. 1–21).

13. What is your opinion of Jacob as you read verses 8–21? Was he trusting the Lord or trusting his own smarts? Explain.

At nightfall Jacob sent his company across the brook Jabbok and remained alone, agitated, and sleepless. "There wrestled a man with him until the breaking of the day" (v. 24).

"Deliver me from the hand of my brother," he had prayed; but Jacob was his own worst enemy and needed deliverance from himself. He had tried too long to live by his wits and trust in himself; he needed to be subdued and conquered and to learn to trust God. That is why the Angel of the Lord (the preincarnate Christ; cf. v. 30) crippled Jacob and then changed his name (vv. 25, 28). He was no longer Jacob, the supplanter, the deceiver; he had become "Israel," one who had fought with God and won the victory by submission and faith in the One Who could bless him.

14. After the wrestling match, Jacob walked with a limp. How has the Lord changed the way you "walk" through life?

Jacob was then ready to meet Esau. The Lord melted Esau's heart, and the two men embraced, kissed, and wept (33:4). After twenty long years, they were reconciled. But they chose not to live together (vv. 16, 17). The spiritual differences between the two brothers were too great for that.

Jacob moved first to Succoth and then to Shechem, where he bought a parcel of ground, spread his tent, and built an altar. He was a worshiping pilgrim, as all true believers are.

Making It Personal

Jacob spent much of his life scheming instead of trusting. However, the Lord had plans for Jacob. He would bless him and make him a blessing to others, and He would not give up on him. First He allowed Jacob to experience the harmful effects of deception in a personal, close-up way. Then He wrestled with Jacob until Jacob submitted to Him.

15. If you feel that the Lord is wrestling with you, will you submit your will and life to Him? If so, how will your walk change?

16. If you need to reconcile with someone, perhaps a close relative, what steps will you take to secure that reconciliation?

Joseph: Dreamer, Slave, Prisoner, and Ruler

Genesis 37; 39—41

"The LORD hath prepared his throne in the heavens; and his kingdom ruleth over all" (Psalm 103:19).

Y ou look just like your father." "You have your mother's beautiful smile." "With those green eyes and red hair, it's easy to tell you're an O'Malley."

You've heard statements like these, haven't you? Often, though, the resemblance between a parent and child may not be simply physical; a son or daughter may also follow a parent's psychological, emotional, or behavioral pattern. Brian's hot temper copies his dad's similar disposition. Julie experiences depression, just as her mother did. Gary swore he would never be an alcoholic like his dad, but now he seems to live for the bottle.

We learn from Genesis that Rebekah favored her son Jacob and that her favoring him led to serious family trouble. At one point Esau, Jacob's brother, wanted to kill Jacob. Years later when Jacob had his own family, he repeated his mother's mistake and favored his son

Joseph over all his other sons. As a result, Joseph's brothers hated him and even plotted to kill him. If God's protecting hand had not shielded Joseph, he would have been the victim of fratricide.

Getting Started

1. In what ways do you resemble your mother or father?

2. How do you explain that some individuals resent a parent's bad habits but repeat them themselves?

Searching the Scriptures

Joseph, Jacob's second youngest son, was born to Rachel when Jacob worked for Laban (Genesis 30:22–24). Rachel gave birth to Joseph's brother Benjamin in Canaan, but she died during labor (35:16–19). Genesis 37:3 reveals that Jacob "loved Joseph more than all his children" and made Joseph "a coat of many colours."

3. How do you think older siblings would feel if their father bought a car only for their seventeen-year-old brother?

One day seventeen-year-old Joseph was tending sheep along with his older brothers, when he caught them in some misconduct and blew the whistle on them to Jacob (37:2). The incident only added fuel to the brothers' hatred of Joseph, "and [they] could not speak peaceably unto him" (v. 4). However, matters were about to get worse.

4. According to verses 5–11, what did Joseph's dreams signify?

5. Agree or disagree: Joseph was arrogant to tell the dreams to his brothers and father. Why?

6. What emotion flared in the brothers upon their hearing about Joseph's dreams?

7. Do you think a believer is wise or unwise to tell others he or she believes the Lord has big plans for him or her? Why?

Joseph's brothers soon found an opportunity to get rid of Joseph. At his father's bidding Joseph went to Shechem to see how things fared with his brothers. Told by a stranger that they had gone to Dothan, he went there and found them. Dothan was an isolated place where the brothers could do with Joseph whatever they chose to do.

The brothers plotted to kill Joseph and to tell their father that a wild beast had devoured him. However, at the advice of brother Reuben, they threw Joseph into a pit. First, though, they stripped him of his multicolored coat. Then at mealtime, when Reuben was absent, they saw a caravan of Ishmaelites passing by and decided to sell Joseph to them (vv. 14–28).

After selling Joseph into slavery, the brothers killed a goat, dipped Joseph's coat in its blood, went home, and showed the bloodstained coat to Jacob as evidence that a savage animal had devoured Joseph. The sight of the coat convinced Jacob that his favorite son was dead. He mourned bitterly, and his sons and daughters tried to comfort him (vv. 29–35).

8. Do you think it is valid to call certain crimes "hate crimes"? Why or why not?

9. With what crime (sin) did the apostle John equate hatred? (See 1 John 3:15.)

10. How can a believer love sinners while hating their sins?

11. What parallels do you see between the way Joseph's brothers treated him and the way Jesus' brethren, the Jews, treated Him?

The traders took Joseph to Egypt, where his circumstances seemed to improve significantly when he was sold to Potiphar, the captain of Pharaoh's bodyguard. He became Potiphar's personal attendant, placed in charge of his house and all of his possessions (Genesis 39:1–6). The Lord was with Joseph. However, Joseph's life soon took a turn that from all human perspectives seemed disastrous, but the Lord did not fail Joseph. He had good plans for him.

12. How has the Lord taught you that disappointment is often His appointment?

Potiphar's wife lusted after Joseph and begged him day after day, "Lie with me." Joseph was in jeopardy. He would not only have to re-sist the temptation to commit fornication, but he would also have to brave the scorn and wrath of a woman rejected. During one attempt to persuade Joseph to sin, Joseph fled from Potiphar's wife, leaving her grasping his garment. She falsely accused him of attempted rape and caused him to be imprisoned. But even while Joseph was in prison, the Lord was with him (vv. 7–21).

13. How do you know the Lord is with you even in life's harshest circumstances?

Instead of indulging in self-pity, Joseph made himself useful, and soon all the prisoners were committed to his charge. However, the years slipped by, and the prospect of his release from prison seemed dim. But God never forsakes His own!

Finally something happened to initiate God's plan for Joseph's release and exaltation. Two important officers of the king had incurred his displeasure and were thrown into prison. Subsequently each officer had a dream, which Joseph interpreted. He told the chief butler that he would be restored to the king's favor in three days but that the chief baker would be executed in three days. Longing for liberty, Joseph urged the butler to plead his case with Pharaoh. But the butler forgot about Joseph (40:23).

Joseph remained in prison until Pharaoh dreamed the dream that would release Joseph from prison and elevate him to the second-highest position in Egypt (41:1–43).

Pharaoh's dream triggered the butler's memory. The butler confessed his forgetfulness and told Pharaoh about Joseph. Pharaoh lost no time in summoning Joseph and relating his dreams of seven fat cows and seven lean cows and seven good ears of grain and seven thin ones. Joseph denied that he could interpret dreams; he was as helpless as Pharaoh's magicians and wise men. Only the true God would give Pharaoh a favorable answer, for it was God Who had caused Pharaoh to dream, and God alone knew what would come to pass.

14. Which characteristics did Joseph show in Egypt that you would like to have in your life?

After interpreting Pharaoh's dream to mean a seven-year famine would follow seven years of plenty, Joseph recommended that Pharaoh appoint someone to supervise the stockpiling of food throughout the land (vv. 33–36). The stored food would be available in the famine years.

Pharaoh knew just the man for the job—Joseph! With the appointment of Joseph to the position of prime minister, Egypt's second in command, God set events in motion that would fulfill the dreams Joseph had had when he was a teenager. He had been a dreamer, a slave, and a prisoner and had become a powerful ruler.

15. How would Joseph's new position fit God's determination to fulfill the Abrahamic Covenant?

Making It Personal

16. As you review your life, how can you see God's hand faithfully guiding you through the rough times as well as the smooth times?

17. How will you show your gratitude for God's faithfulness to you?

18. What have you learned from Joseph's life that you can apply to your own life?

Joseph's Dreams Come True

Genesis 42:1—47:12

"Put on therefore, as the elect of God, holy and beloved, bowels of mercies, kindness, humbleness of mind, meekness, longsuffering; forbearing one another, and forgiving one another, if any man have a quarrel against any: even as Christ forgave you, so also do ye" (Colossians 3:12, 13).

Occasionally TV news broadcasts take a break from reporting crime, uprisings, wars, and rumors of wars to share the happy news that long-separated family members have been reunited. Sometimes the family members are adult siblings who were separated in their childhood because they were placed in foster care after their parents died. One news story featured three brothers in their seventies who met for the first time in sixty years. Although they didn't recognize one another, they joyfully embraced. Their sense of family quickly erased the sadness of their long separation.

Getting Started

1. What is the longest time you have been separated from a parent or sibling?

2. What three words best describe how you felt when you and your parent or sibling were reunited?

As we conclude our study of Genesis, we are privileged to witness a family reunion. After many long years of separation from his father and brothers, Joseph was reunited with them. First he met his brothers in a tense situation, but his tears of joy confirmed his love for them. Then he and his father were reunited, and the family circle was complete.

Searching the Scriptures

Sometimes God turns the worst times into the best times. He allowed Joseph to experience rejection, slavery, and imprisonment before he experienced honor and recognition. Next He used a famine to bring about the reunion of Joseph and his family. Truly God works in mysterious ways to perform His wonders, and often His blessings follow life's bleakest times.

The famine struck with a vengeance. It was "over all the face of the earth." Because grain was available only in Egypt, people from all countries went to Joseph to buy grain. Joseph's family was no exception. Thus in the providence of God, Jacob sent Joseph's ten older brothers to purchase grain from their brother Joseph, whom they would not recognize. Jacob kept Benjamin home, because he feared for his safety (Genesis 41:56—42:4).

Joseph recognized his brothers when they bowed low before him, and he spoke harshly to them. He asked where they had come from, accused them of spying, and put them in prison for three days.

Twenty years before, the brothers had committed an atrocious crime against Joseph. Now three days in an Egyptian jail and Joseph's demand that one of them remain as a hostage until the others brought Benjamin to Egypt awakened their consciences. They confessed in their native language in Joseph's presence, "We are verily guilty concerning our brother, in that we saw the anguish of his soul, when he besought us, and we would not hear; therefore is this distress come upon us." Reuben went so far as to tell the others in effect, "I told you so. It's payback time for what we did to Joseph" (vv. 6–22).

Of course the brothers didn't think the Egyptian ruler (Joseph) understood what they were saying, but he did. Their remorseful words opened his heart toward them. He left the men momentarily and wept (v. 24).

3. Do you agree or disagree that Joseph's brothers' consciences had troubled them for twenty years? Why?

4. How do you explain that a conscience may trouble one guilty person but not trouble another guilty person in the least?

5. Why is a conscience not necessarily an indicator of right and wrong?

Joseph detained Simeon in Egypt while the other brothers returned to Canaan to give their sad report to their father (vv. 24–34). Twenty years earlier, they had inflicted an injury on Jacob from which he had never fully recovered. Now they added to his sorrow by telling him that Simeon was a hostage in Egypt and that Benjamin must accompany them on their next trip to buy grain. Our sins bring grief not only to ourselves but also to those whom we deeply love. Jacob believed that "all these things are against me" (v. 36).

6. What sins are especially injurious to family members?

7. Why is there no such thing as a victimless crime?

Jacob delayed sending his sons again to Egypt to buy food. He resolutely determined that Benjamin "my son shall not go down with you; for his brother is dead, and he is left alone: if mischief befall him by the way in which ye go, then shall ye bring down my gray hairs with sorrow to the grave" (v. 38).

8. Why was Benjamin so dear to Jacob (Genesis 35:16–18)?

Judah pleaded with his father to let Benjamin go so "that we may live, and not die," and he pledged himself as a guarantee of Benjamin's safe return (43:8, 9). Jacob hoped that God Almighty would grant them mercy, but he was pessimistic. He acquiesced, "And if I be bereaved of my children, I am bereaved" (v. 14).

9. How can you keep from having a pessimistic attitude when you pray about a desperate situation?

Upon their return to Egypt, Joseph's brothers received an invitation to dine with him (vv. 16, 17). Further, they were astonished when they were seated in the exact order of their ages (v. 33). How much did "that man" know about them? Surely they trembled, and their awakened consciences must have added to their fears.

Joseph, the host, inquired about the brothers' father. Was he in good health? Then when he saw Benjamin, he could hardly restrain his emotions. He went to his room and wept. After washing away his tears, he returned to the meal (vv. 29–31).

Joseph released Simeon and allowed all eleven brothers to leave for Canaan. They could hardly believe how well things had turned out. The lord of Egypt had royally entertained them, and their sacks were bulging with grain. How pleased Jacob, their father, would be! Then lightning struck.

According to Genesis 44:4–6, Joseph's steward caught up with the brothers and accused them of stealing Joseph's silver cup. He searched, finding in Benjamin's sack the cup that Joseph had planted (v. 12).

10. Read verses 14–34. Using about twenty words, summarize Judah's plea for Benjamin's life.

Ordering the Egyptians from the room, Joseph unashamedly and loudly wept. "I am Joseph," he told his brothers. They were astonished and troubled and could not speak.

Joseph did not even consider revenge. He believed God had overruled their evil deed for Joseph's good and theirs. And their penitence had secured God's forgiveness and Joseph's as well (45:2–8).

11. Why do you think Joseph could not restrain himself after hearing Judah's plea?

12. How does it encourage you to know that God places His people strategically so they may fulfill His purposes?

13. How does knowing that God orchestrated the events in Joseph's life help you face *your* daily life?

Joseph commissioned his brothers to fetch Jacob to Egypt, and he promised to let his family settle in the region of Goshen (45:9, 10). The brothers returned to Canaan and related the good news to their father. It revived Jacob's spirit, and he accompanied his sons and their children to Egypt (45:24—46:7).

Joseph and his father met in Goshen and embraced each other with tears of joy. At long last Jacob was at peace. Jacob confessed to Pharaoh that his life had been a pilgrimage (47:9).

14. How do you view your journey through life? Why?

Making It Personal

Can you identify with Joseph by seeing God's providential hand in your life? Although life's journey has probably been rough at times, God has guided you and placed you where you can honor Him.

15. How will you maximize your effectiveness for God this week?

More than likely in your life, someone has treated you unjustly, just as Joseph's brothers treated him unjustly. However, Joseph held no grudges. He freely forgave his brothers. Do you need to forgive someone?

16. Whom do you need to forgive?

17. How will you tell that person that you forgive him or her?